LIVING ON MARS

by Ruth Owen

Consultants:

Suzy Gazlay, MA
Recipient, Presidential Award for Excellence in Science Teaching

Kevin Yates
Fellow of the Royal Astronomical Society

Ruby Tuesday Books

Published in 2015 by Ruby Tuesday Books Ltd.

Copyright © 2015 Ruby Tuesday Books Ltd.

Editor: Mark J. Sachner
Designer: Emma Randall
Production: John Lingham

Photo Credits:
Alamy: 22; ESA/IPMB: 19 (top); European Space Agency: 11, 18, 19 (bottom), 27 (top); NASA: 4–5, 6–7, 8–9, 10, 12, 14–15, 16–17, 24, 26, 27 (bottom), 28–29, 31; NASA Ames Research Center/Eric James: 13; Shutterstock: Cover, 25; Superstock: 23; Wikipedia Creative Commons: 20–21.).

Library of Congress Control Number: 2013920130

ISBN 978-1-909673-50-2

Printed and published in the United States of America

For further information including rights and permissions requests, please contact our Customer Service Department at 877-337-8577.

CONTENTS

Explorers and Settlers

Throughout human history, people have been explorers and settlers.

We have explored jungles and climbed mountains. We have traveled long distances to find new places to live. We haven't only explored our home **planet**. Astronauts blasted off from Earth to explore the Moon. Today, astronauts even live in space aboard the International Space Station, or ISS.

Scientists on Earth work with the astronauts aboard the ISS. Together, they study what happens to people when they live in space.

So what's next? The answer is to explore and settle on another planet. The most likely planet for humans to visit is Mars. Around the world, scientists are working on plans to send astronauts to this faraway world. One day, humans might even live on Mars!

Mars TO DO list

Scientists and engineers have a lot to figure out before humans can visit Mars.

- Design a spacecraft
- Design a protective spacesuit
- Design a Mars home
- Invent a way to get oxygen
- Invent a way to get water
- Figure out how to grow food
- Design Mars vehicles
- Invent ways to get fuel and energy
- Choose and train astronauts

Welcome to Mars

Mars is one of Earth's closest neighbors in space. It's still a very long way away, though!

The closest Earth and Mars ever get is 35 million miles (56 million km) apart. Usually, however, the two planets are much farther apart. Earth and Mars are both **orbiting**, or moving around, the Sun. Each planet is moving on its own pathway, though. So the distance between the two planets changes all the time.

The surface of Mars looks like a dusty, rocky desert. The soil is reddish-brown because it contains lots of rust. The red soil gives Mars its nickname of the Red Planet. There are no oceans, lakes, or rivers on Mars. There is frozen water on the planet, though.

Earth: 7,918 miles (12,743 km)

Mars: 4,212 miles (6,779 km)

Mars is home to a giant volcano called Olympus Mons.
It is 14 miles (22.5 km) high.

Mars has a canyon called Valles Marineris. It is eight times
longer and three times deeper than the Grand Canyon.

An Extreme New World

Human bodies are designed to live on Earth. The extreme conditions on Mars will be very dangerous for human explorers.

Mars is an extremely cold planet. That's because it is farther from the Sun than Earth. Also, Earth is surrounded by a thick layer of gases called an **atmosphere**. Earth's atmosphere traps the Sun's warmth on Earth. Mars has only a very thin atmosphere. So heat escapes from the planet. Sometimes, temperatures on Mars drop to -190°F (-123°C).

The Sun produces a type of energy called **radiation**. Too much radiation can cause cancer and other diseases. Earth is surrounded by an area called the **magnetosphere** that helps block radiation. Mars does not have this protection. So the high amounts of radiation on Mars will be harmful to humans.

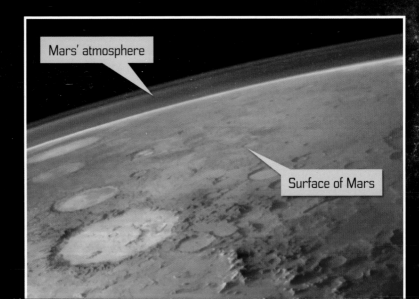

Mars' atmosphere

Surface of Mars

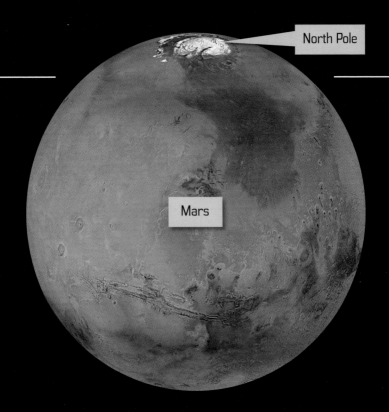

North Pole

Mars

Ice at the North Pole on Mars

A Dangerous World

A human on Mars will need protection from cold and radiation. There are other dangers, too.

The air on Earth contains oxygen that humans need to breathe. The air on Mars contains almost no oxygen. It is mostly made up of poisonous carbon dioxide gas.

Scientists and engineers must design spacesuits for astronauts to wear on Mars. Astronauts will also need protective habitats, or buildings. The spacesuits and habitats will protect astronauts from radiation and the cold. They will also supply the astronauts with oxygen at all times.

This illustration shows how habitats on the surface of Mars might look.

This scientist is wearing a test spacesuit. Astronauts on Mars will wear something that looks like this.

The First Explorers

Before astronauts visit Mars, other explorers may go on ahead.

These explorers will not need oxygen, protective suits, or habitats. That's because they will be robots.

In the future, robots could explore Mars to find the best place to build a settlement. The *K10* robot is a scout, or explorer, robot. At the moment, it is being tested on Earth. A robot scout like *K10* could send photos, videos, and other information back to Earth. Scientists would use this information to plan a **mission** to Mars.

Robots might even deliver equipment to Mars and set it up. Then it will be ready for future human explorers.

There are already robots studying the surface of Mars. This robot is named *Curiosity*. It measured how much radiation there is on the surface of Mars. It sent this important information back to Earth.

An engineer carries out tests with a *K10* robot.

Mission to Mars

The first human mission to Mars is likely to include a small **crew** of just four people.

The astronauts would fly to Mars in a spacecraft. The spacecraft would then orbit around the planet. The astronauts might make several visits to the planet's surface. They would travel down to the surface in a landing craft. After a few hours exploring, they would return to their spacecraft. After about a month in orbit, the crew would fly back to Earth.

Rocket

A spacecraft heading for Mars may blast off aboard a rocket similar to the one in this illustration.

Several missions to explore the planet might take place over 10 or 20 years. Then, the building of a Mars base camp might begin. Many journeys to Mars would be needed to deliver equipment and building materials.

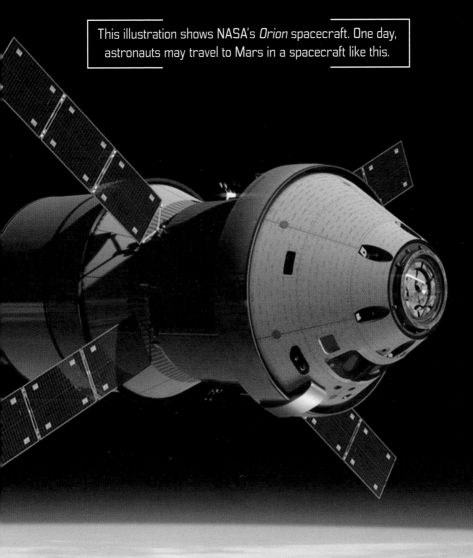

This illustration shows NASA's *Orion* spacecraft. One day, astronauts may travel to Mars in a spacecraft like this.

A round trip to Mars would take about 17 months. No human has ever spent this long in space. So how will it affect an astronaut's body?

One big danger to the astronauts is the lack of **gravity** in space. Gravity is the force that pulls things toward the center of a planet. Human bodies are designed to live on Earth, where there is strong gravity. Without gravity, a person's body is weightless. This makes bones and muscles become weak. On the way to Mars, astronauts will live without gravity for many months. Their bodies might be badly damaged. When they return to Earth, they may not be able to walk.

An astronaut on the International Space Station shows how objects float in zero gravity.

Astronauts on the ISS exercise for at least two hours every day. This helps lessen the harmful effects of weightlessness.

Astronauts who travel to Mars will be trapped inside a tiny spacecraft for months. They may become bored, unhappy, and homesick.

Scientists wanted to test how people will cope. So in 2010, a six-member crew carried out a **simulation**, or pretend Mars mission. The mission was called Mars500. The six Marsonauts were shut into a simulated spacecraft. They lived in the spacecraft for 520 days. The men lived exactly as they would in space. They carried out experiments. They made daily checks on their spacecraft. They could only contact the outside world by radio or email.

Scientists studied how the mission affected the crew's bodies. They also studied how it affected their minds.

This is the Mars500 crew inside their simulated spacecraft.

The Marsonauts made simulated visits to a pretend surface of Mars. They wore spacesuits. They also followed safety rules that real astronauts will follow.

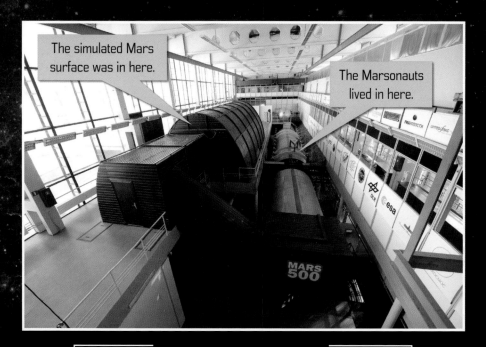

The simulated Mars surface was in here.

The Marsonauts lived in here.

The Mars500 mission did not leave Earth. The simulated spacecraft stayed on the ground in Russia.

Mars on Earth

One day, people may live and work on Mars.

Scientists need to know what that will be like.
So they have created simulated Mars base camps on
Earth. One of the camps is in the Arctic in Nunavut,
Canada. This area is the most Mars-like place on
Earth. A second camp is in a rocky desert in Utah.
Here the land is very similar to the dusty, rocky
surface of Mars.

Scientists live at the camps for weeks or months
at a time. They must live as if they are on Mars.
Each crew member is given an exact
amount of food and water. They cannot
leave the living habitats without
a spacesuit.

This is the simulated Mars
habitat in the Arctic. It has
a work area, a living area,
and a kitchen. There are also
crew rooms with bunks, a
shower, and a toilet.

FLAG INE MARS ARCTIC RESEARCH STATION

Members of the crew leave the habitat to do experiments on the rocks and soil.
They test out tools and equipment that may one day be used on Mars.

A Home on Mars

The first homes on Mars will probably be small habitats on the surface. The habitats will be sent to Mars on spacecraft.

Many years from now, people may want to build a larger, more permanent settlement. This type of settlement might be built underground.

Scientists think there are underground tunnels called lava tubes on Mars. When lava erupts from a volcano, it flows over the ground. Then it cools, hardens, and turns to rock. Sometimes, empty tube-like spaces form inside the rock. An underground Mars settlement could be built inside one of these lava tubes.

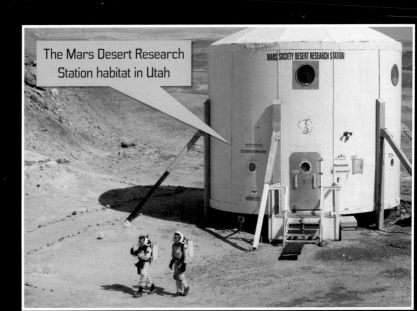

The Mars Desert Research Station habitat in Utah

This is an underground lava tube on Earth. Living in an underground home on Mars would give people protection from the radiation and cold.

Survival Essentials

To survive on Mars, humans will need water, oxygen, and energy.

Billions of years ago, there was liquid water on Mars. Then Mars became much colder. Today, there is only frozen water on Mars. Most of this ice is underground. Robots could search for places where the ground contains ice. The ice could then be removed from the ground and turned back into water.

People living on Mars could recycle water. For example, water used for washing can be cleaned and turned back into fresh water. In this photo, astronauts on the International Space Station are drinking water that was once urine!

Water is made up of hydrogen and oxygen. So settlers on Mars can separate the hydrogen from the oxygen. Then the oxygen can be pumped into habitats and spacesuits for people to breathe.

One type of energy that a Mars settlement will use is **solar power**. Solar energy comes from the Sun, and it can be turned into electricity. This will be used for lighting, heating, and powering equipment.

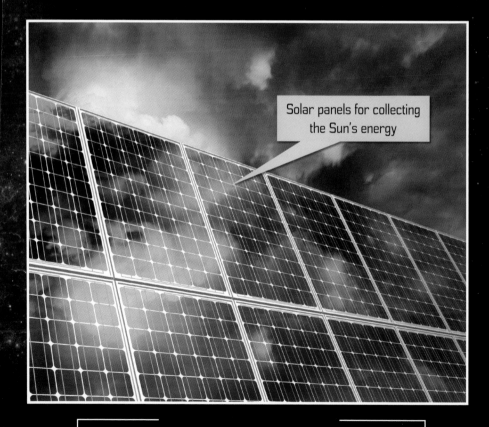

Solar panels for collecting the Sun's energy

Mars receives less sunshine than Earth. There is still enough solar energy to be used for power, though.

Growing Food on Mars

When astronauts make short visits to Mars, they will take food with them.

Once people settle on Mars, sending food from Earth will be too expensive. So plants and seeds will be sent to Mars. Then people in a Mars settlement will grow their own food.

Plants could not survive on the surface of Mars without protection. So crops will be grown inside. The plants will not be grown in soil. That's because the soil on Mars is very toxic. Instead, they will grow in a special liquid made from water. This liquid will contain all the **nutrients** the plants need.

Trail mix

Creamed spinach

Crackers

Beef patty

Cheese spread

Candy-coated peanuts

Cashew nuts

Orange Ade

Steak

Orange drink

Astronauts eat long-lasting, packaged foods like these when they are in space.

The greenhouse inside the Mars500 simulated spacecraft

Just like humans, plants, such as lettuce and onions, are designed to live on Earth. Scientists are investigating how well plants will grow on Mars.

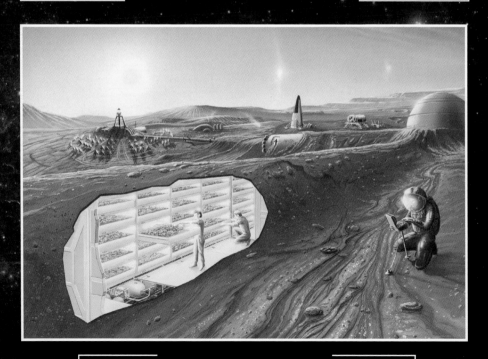

This illustration shows a future Mars settlement. The cutaway section shows crops being grown underground.

Humans or Martians?

Why do people want to explore and settle on Mars? There are many answers to that question.

Mars could become a rest stop for spacecraft traveling from Earth to more distant places. One day, we may need a new home if Earth is no longer a safe place to live. Maybe there's an answer that is even more simple. It may be that humans are inventors and explorers.

Earth

This photograph shows what Earth looks like from Mars.
The photo was taken by the robot *Curiosity*.

Organizations such as NASA and the European Space Agency are working on plans to send astronauts to Mars. So are companies run by business people.

From Earth, we can see Mars as a bright dot in the night sky. Perhaps some day soon, a human will stand on Mars and see Earth in the same way!

People on Mars will use radios and computers to communicate with Earth. It can take up to 20 minutes for a message to travel from one planet to the other.

Phobos

Deimos

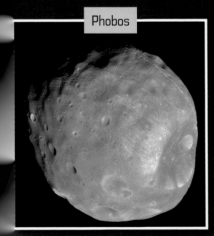
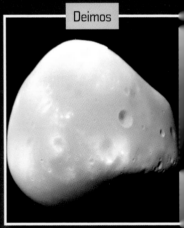

Mars has two small moons. From the planet's surface, they look like tiny bright spots in the night sky.

Glossary

atmosphere (AT-muh-sfeer)
A layer of gases around a planet, moon, or star.

crew (KROO)
A group of people who work together to get a job done, such as on a train, ship, plane, ambulance, or spacecraft.

gravity (GRAV-uh-tee)
The force that pulls things toward the center of large objects, such as planets and stars. Gravity keeps things from drifting into space.

magnetosphere (mag-NEE-tuh-sfeer)
An area around Earth that acts like the magnetic field around a magnet. The magnetosphere traps radiation from the Sun and stops it from reaching Earth.

mission (MISH-uhn)
An important task or series of tasks carried out for a particular purpose.

nutrient (NOO-tree-uhnt)
A substance needed by a living thing in order for it to grow, get energy, and stay healthy.

orbiting (OR-bit-ing)
Moving around another object.

planet (PLAN-et)
A large object in space that is orbiting a star. Some planets in our solar system, such as Mars and Earth, are made of rock. Others, such as Jupiter and Uranus, are made of gases and liquids.

radiation (ray-dee-AY-shuhn)
A type of invisible energy that travels through space in waves. The Sun releases this type of energy.

simulation (sim-yoo-LAY-shuhn)
Carrying out tasks in a pretend situation. A simulation is often used to teach people how to do something so that one day they can do it for real.

solar power (SOH-lur POW-ur)
Power, such as electricity, that is created using energy from the Sun.

Index

Read More

Lawrence, Ellen. *Mars: The Dusty Planet (Zoom Into Space)*. New York: Ruby Tuesday Books (2014).

Nelson, Maria. *Life on the International Space Station (Extreme Jobs in Extreme Places)*. New York: Gareth Stevens Publishing (2013).

Learn More Online

To learn more about living on Mars, go to
www.rubytuesdaybooks.com/livingonmars